The Science of Living Things

What is a
Primate?

Bobbie Kalman & Heather Levigne

Crabtree Publishing Company

The Science of Living Things Series
A Bobbie Kalman Book

To David
who loves and inspires me

Editor-in-Chief
Bobbie Kalman

Writing team
Bobbie Kalman
Heather Levigne

Managing editor
Lynda Hale

Editors
Jane Lewis
Kate Calder
Hannelore Sotzek
John Crossingham

Computer design
Lynda Hale

Production coordinator
Hannelore Sotzek

Photographs
Wolfgang Kaehler: page 24 (bottom left)
Tom Stack and Associates:
    Nancy Adams: pages 18, 23 (top); Larry Lipsky: page 13 (top);
    Joe McDonald: pages 10 (top), 11 (top); Gary Milburn: pages
    5, 27 (both), 28 (top); Mark Newman: page 4; Denise Tackett:
    pages 22, 28 (bottom); Larry Tackett: page 26 (both); Roy Toft:
    pages 3, 9, 10 (bottom), 11 (bottom), 14, 19 (top), 31 (top)
Michael Turco: front cover, title page, pages 8, 12, 13 (bottom),
    15, 17 (top & bottom), 19 (bottom), 21 (top), 24 (top),
    25 (both), 30
Art Wolfe: pages 16, 20, 21 (bottom), 23 (bottom),
    24 (bottom right), 29, 31 (bottom)
Other images by Digital Stock and Eyewire, Inc.

Illustrations
Barbara Bedell: pages 5 (bottom), 22

Separations and film
Dot 'n Line Image Inc.

Printer
Worzalla Publishing Company

Crabtree Publishing Company

350 Fifth Avenue
Suite 3308
New York
N.Y. 10118

360 York Road, RR 4,
Niagara-on-the-Lake,
Ontario, Canada
L0S 1J0

73 Lime Walk
Headington
Oxford OX3 7AD
United Kingdom

Cataloging in Publication Data

Kalman, Bobbie
    What is a primate?

(The science of living things)
Includes index.

ISBN 0-86505-922-5 (library bound) ISBN 0-86505-950-0 (pbk.)
This book examines the physiology, feeding and reproductive habits,
and social behavior of each group of primates, including chimpanzees,
orangutans, gorillas, gibbons, Old World and New World monkeys,
marmosets, and humans.

1. Primates—Juvenile literature. [1. Primates.] I. Levigne, Heather.
II. Title. III. Series: Kalman, Bobbie. Science of living things.

QL737.P9K245 1999   j599.8   LC 99-13164
                                               CIP

Contents

What is a primate?

Monkeys, apes, lemurs, and humans all belong to a group of living things called **primates**. Primates are **mammals**. A mammal's body has fur or hair, which keeps the animal warm when it is cold and helps it stay cool when it is hot.

Chimpanzees are our closest living relatives in the animal kingdom.

Brain power

Primates are intelligent animals. They have a large brain. Primates such as chimpanzees and capuchins can learn how to use rocks and twigs as tools. Some chimps and gorillas have even been trained to add numbers or use sign language.

Family life

Most primates live in families. Some live in pairs, and others live in **troops** of up to 100 members. Family members care for and protect one another. How many members are there in your family?

(right) Ring-tailed lemurs are small primates that are about the size of a house cat.

Primates are the only mammals that have hands. Each hand has four fingers and one thumb. The palms are hairless and sensitive to touch.

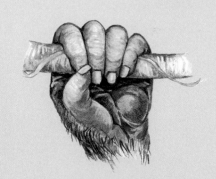

*A primate's hand is **prehensile**, or able to grasp. Primates use their hands to pick up objects or hold onto branches. Many have prehensile feet as well.*

Other mammals have paws that are not prehensile. They do not have a thumb. Unlike primates, these animals cannot grasp objects.

The primate family tree

Scientists believe that primates **evolved** from a small mammal that lived in trees. The brain, skull, muscles, and **reproductive system** of this ancestor were similar to those of primates today.

Different types

There are over 200 species of primates. They are divided into two groups—**prosimians** and **anthropoids**. Tarsiers, lemurs, lorises, and bush babies are prosimians. Humans, apes, monkeys, marmosets, and tamarins are anthropoids.

A monkey or an ape?

Do you know the difference between an ape and a monkey? A simple way to tell is to look for a tail—monkeys have tails, whereas apes do not. Most monkeys are smaller than apes and spend more time in trees.

Smallest and biggest

The tiniest primate is the mouse lemur, which weighs less than three ounces (85 g). It is small enough to fit in the palm of your hand! Gorillas are the largest primates. A gorilla can weigh up to 380 pounds (172 kg).

*Chimpanzees, bonobos, orangutans, and gorillas, shown above, are called **great apes**. They are the largest primates.*

Prosimians, such as this crowned lemur, are the smallest of all the primates. They live in trees.

(left) **New World monkeys** such as this spider monkey have a prehensile tail that they use for holding onto tree branches.

(below) Humans are the most intelligent primates. We have larger brains than monkeys and apes, and we are able to learn more.

(above) Gibbons are known as **lesser apes**. They are smaller than great apes, and they spend most of their time in trees.

(right) Mandrill baboons are **Old World monkeys.** They have **sitting pads,** and their tail is not prehensile.

A primate's body

A primate's body is suited to its **habitat**, or home. Many primates have small, lightweight bodies that allow them to move easily among the trees. Larger, heavier primates such as chimpanzees and gorillas spend most of their time on the ground.

As some primates grow older, the hair that covers their body gets gray. Some primates even lose their hair and go bald!

Some primates can walk on two legs just as humans do. Most apes **knuckle-walk**, using all four limbs.

Thumbs up!

Look at your hand and see how you are able to wiggle your thumb and fingers separately. Primates are the only animals that have hands with **opposable** thumbs. Our thumbs allow us to pick up and hold objects. Animals without opposable thumbs cannot do this. Try to pick up an apple and eat it without using your thumb. It is hard to do!

*All primates have eyes that face forward to give them **three-dimensional** vision.*

Most primates have long arms and shorter legs. Some, however, are long legged. This lemur, shown right, uses its long legs for leaping.

Some primates have a long, strong tail that they use for balance or to grasp tree branches.

Many prosimians have a long, doglike snout. They use their sense of smell to locate one another, find food, and sense danger.

Get my message?

Animals have many ways of **communicating**, or giving messages to one another. Primates use sounds, **gestures**, **body language**, and **facial expressions** to show members of their troop and others how they feel. Some primates can make the sounds that humans make. They sneeze, burp, hiccup, and even laugh!

Gorilla talk

Gorillas use many sounds to "talk" to one another. Female gorillas grunt to scold their young. The leader of a group makes hooting and grunting sounds to call the other members of the group and keep them together.

When primates are excited, they make sure everyone knows it! Gorillas, like the one above, stand on two legs and beat their chest with their hands. They run around slapping the ground while making loud hooting noises. The lion-tailed macaque, shown right, bares its sharp teeth and screams when it is excited.

Communicating with touch

Many primates use touch to communicate. Chimpanzees and bonobos greet one another by hugging and back slapping. Mothers hold their babies to help protect them and make them feel safe. Primates also **groom** one another to show affection. They gather in groups to pick dirt and lice from one another's fur.

Body language

Primates use body language to show how they are feeling. They send messages to one another by making gestures and facial expressions. When chimpanzees are nervous or upset, for example, they make a wide grin that shows all their teeth. This "smile" is called a **fear grin**.

(above) This young olive baboon sits quietly as its mother cleans its fur.

(left) To show respect for its elder, this young bonobo turns away from the adult. The older ape makes a friendly gesture by touching the younger bonobo's back.

Chimpanzees

Young chimpanzees like to play. Playing helps them learn how to communicate with the members of their troop.

Chimpanzees live in large groups that can have up to 80 members. They are very **sociable** animals—they enjoy the company of other chimps. When they meet chimps they know, they greet one another by grooming, touching hands, kissing, and hugging.

R-E-S-P-E-C-T

Adult males are the leaders of a chimpanzee troop. The other chimpanzees treat them with great respect. Females also gain respect from the troop as they grow older and have babies. Young chimps are the least respected but must show respect to all members of their troop.

Clever hunters

Although chimpanzees eat mainly fruit and plants, they also eat meat. Male chimps hunt in groups to catch monkeys, bush pigs, and young antelopes. Several members of the group chase their **prey**, and others herd it into a trap. When they have caught an animal, the male chimps are the first to eat. Females with babies feed afterward.

Chimpanzees often make funny faces! They have many of the same expressions as people. What do you think this chimpanzee is thinking?

Using tools

Chimps are skilled at using tools, especially when they need to find food. They poke sticks into trees and insect homes to reach their prey inside. Some use stones to crack open nuts and fruit. To get a drink of water, chimpanzees chew a mouthful of leaves and then use them as a sponge to soak up rainwater from tree holes. Chimps also use objects for self-defense. If they feel threatened by another animal, they will throw rocks at it.

A twig makes a good "fishing rod" for catching insects! A chimp pokes a twig into the ground so insects will crawl onto the stick. When it pulls out the twig, the chimp licks off the tasty treat. Yum!

Bonobos

Bonobos look like chimpanzees and greet one other with handshakes and hugs just as chimps do. Bonobos are different from chimpanzees in many ways, however. A bonobo has a thinner body, smaller head, and darker face than a chimp. Chimpanzees sometimes fight with one another, whereas bonobos are more peaceful.

Females are the leaders in bonobo families. When young female bonobos become adults, they leave their family in order to start a new one of their own. Most male bonobos, however, stay in the same troop for life.

Bonobos, shown above, search for food together and share their meals. Bonobos walk upright and look similar to people.

This little bonobo is tasting a reed. Babies watch how their mother chooses food in order to learn which plants are good to eat. Bonobos eat up to 300 types of fruit, leaves, and other plants.

Orangutans

Orangutans are the only great apes that live in trees. Their name means "person of the forest" in **Malay**, the language of Malaysia. Orangutans do not spend much time on the ground. Even though they are large, they live in the **canopy**, or top layer of the forest. They move carefully from tree to tree. Orangutans are not daredevils like some primates, such as gibbons (see page 20).

Baby orangutans stay close to their mother until they are old enough to climb trees and find food without her help.

Leave me alone!

Orangutans are **solitary** animals—they live alone. Mothers, however, live with their babies for up to eight years. Orangutans prefer not to share their meals. Although male orangutans do not usually fight, they will use their large size to **intimidate**, or scare, others away from their food.

People used to think that apes were afraid of water, but orangutans like to swim!

The long call

Male orangutans make a lot of noise in the morning. They grumble and roar loudly so other orangutans will hear them up to a mile away! A pouch of skin under their chin swells up and **amplifies** their **long call**, or loud sounds. Orangutans make long calls to let others know where they are so they can avoid one another.

Male orangutans have large cheek flaps and long hair that make them appear larger.

Shhh...this orangutan is going to sleep above the ground in a nest made of branches and leaves.

Gorillas

Many people believe that gorillas are ferocious beasts, but they are actually gentle animals. Gorillas live in small families of five to twenty members. An adult male leads the troop, which includes at least two adult females and their babies. He keeps a close watch over the members to help protect them from danger. Although few animals prey on gorillas, sometimes leopards are able to catch young or old ones that cannot move quickly.

*When male gorillas are between eight and twelve years old, they are called **blackbacks**. As male gorillas grow older, the fur on their back turns gray or silver, and they are called **silverbacks**. The gorilla shown above is a silverback.*

A big appetite

Gorillas are **folivores**, which means they eat mainly the leaves and stems of plants such as bamboo and wild celery. Gorillas have a large body and need a lot of **energy** to breathe and grow. Leaves do not provide as much energy as insects or meat, so gorillas have to spend most of their time foraging for food. Gorillas search for food within their **home range**, or territory. Their home range is a vast area. It has to be big enough to provide food for the entire troop.

Baby gorillas need a lot of attention after they are born. They cling to their mother's back for two to three years so she can care for them easily.

Gorillas build nests on the ground for sleeping. They can build a nest of branches and leaves in thirty seconds. Gorillas can have breakfast in bed because their long arms can reach for food near their nest.

Gibbons

Gibbons make up a group of primates known as the lesser apes. They are the smallest species of ape. Like great apes, gibbons can stand upright on two legs, but they spend most of their time high up in the trees, swinging from branch to branch.

Go, gibbon, go!

Gibbons are the only primates whose main method of movement is **brachiation**. They hang from a branch with one hand and swing their body forward to grab a second branch with the other hand.

Watch me fly!

Gibbons have long, strong arms. Their wrist bones allow them to twist and rotate their body as they swing quickly from branch to branch. Sometimes gibbons travel so quickly that they let go of one branch and fly through the air toward the next one!

A gibbon's arms are much longer than its legs. When a gibbon walks on the ground, it holds its arms up in the air to prevent them from dragging on the ground!

What a racket!

In the early morning, gibbons sing loud duets with their mates to defend their territory from gibbons in other troops. A female gibbon makes hooting calls that are answered by a nearby female. The two families move closer until they can see one another. Then the males begin hooting and whooping to scare away the other family. Gibbons do not usually fight. After a while, each family returns to its own territory.

(right) Siamangs are the largest type of gibbon. They use the pouch of skin on their throat to make a booming noise. The sound warns other gibbons to stay away from their territory.

(below) Gibbons mate for life. Unlike most male apes, male gibbons help care for their young and teach them how to walk, swing in the trees, and behave within the group.

Old World monkeys

The monkeys of Asia and Africa are known as Old World monkeys. The term Old World refers to Africa, Asia, and Europe.

Old World monkeys make up the largest group of primates. They live in almost every kind of natural habitat. Their bodies have **adapted**, or changed over time, to suit different climates and environments. In forested areas, Old World monkeys spend most of their time in trees. Other species such as baboons live on the open **savannahs**, or grasslands, of Africa.

Colobus monkeys, shown left, live high in the treetops and rarely come down to the ground.

Different diets

Old World monkeys are either folivores or **omnivores**. Omnivores eat both plants and animals and have one large stomach. Folivores eat leaves, which are hard to **digest**. To help them absorb their food more easily, their stomach has four parts. The food they eat is broken down slowly as it passes through each stomach area.

A proboscis monkey has an unusual-looking nose, which is long and hangs down over its mouth. When a male proboscis monkey becomes angry or excited, its nose swells and turns red!

*When Old World monkeys rest or sleep, they sit upright rather than lie down. Many have sitting pads, called **ischial callosities**, on their bottom. These monkeys carry this comfortable sitting cushion wherever they go!*

New World monkeys

New World monkeys live in South and Central America. An obvious difference between New World and Old World monkeys is right in the middle of their face! New World monkeys have flat noses with wide nostrils that point sideways, whereas Old World monkeys' nostrils are close together and point downward. New World monkeys do not have sitting pads. They also do not have opposable thumbs for grasping—these monkeys use their big toes to grip tree branches.

New World monkeys spend their entire life in trees. Howler monkeys, spider monkeys, capuchins, wooly monkeys, sakis, uakaris, and titis all belong to this group.

The monkey on the left is a capuchin, and the one on the right is a douc langur. Do you know which is an Old World monkey and which is a New World monkey? Here's a hint—the nose knows!

Look, mom—five hands!

New World monkeys have a prehensile tail, which they use as an extra limb for grasping branches. The tip of their tail has a sensitive patch of skin that looks like the palm of a hand. This patch helps the monkey get a better grip on tree branches. New World monkeys can hang from their feet and tail and use both hands to reach for fruit.

(top right) The capuchin is one of the more common New World monkeys. It is found in most forested areas of South America, where it swings and leaps from tree to tree.

(right) At dawn, howler monkeys make loud, roaring calls. These sounds warn other monkeys in the area to stay away from their territory.

Prosimians

All prosimians, except lemurs, are **nocturnal**—they sleep during the day and are active mainly at night. Nocturnal living helps these small primates survive among larger primates such as monkeys. When prosimians and monkeys compete for the same food, the bigger, smarter monkeys usually win. By hunting while the monkeys are sleeping, prosimians avoid competing for food.

What's that smell?

Many prosimians mark their territory by leaving a strong scent on trees and leaves. Male lemurs have **glands** on their wrists that release a scent. They use this scent to warn other males to stay away. Bush babies rub their urine on their hands and feet in order to leave their scent everywhere they go. This scent informs other prosimians that the marked area is already occupied.

Leaping lemurs

Lemurs have strong hind legs that help them leap among trees. They live on the island of Madagascar, where there are no larger primates to threaten them. Lemurs are the only prosimians that are **diurnal**. They are active mainly during the day, and they do not have to compete for food.

Lorises crawl slowly on all four feet. They eat insects such as caterpillars, which cannot outrun them!

Lemurs such as this red ruffed lemur make loud calls to communicate with the members of their troop.

Tiny tarsiers

Tarsiers may look cute and harmless, but they are actually **predators**! They eat other animals such as insects, lizards, birds, rodents, and snakes. Tarsiers have large eyes that help them see in the dark.

Li'l bitty bush babies

Bush babies are also called galagos. They eat insects. In winter, when insects are scarce, they scrape the bark off trees and lick the tree sap inside. Bush babies are the most agile prosimians. They escape predators by running and leaping from tree to tree at high speeds.

Tarsiers can rotate their head 180 degrees—far enough to see what is directly behind them.

Bush babies can move their ears in opposite directions at the same time. Their sensitive hearing helps them locate nearby insects in the dark.

Marmosets and tamarins

Marmosets and tamarins have similar fingers and toes. All their digits, except their big toes, are tipped with sharp, pointed nails that resemble claws. These sharp nails help marmosets and tamarins grip tree branches.

The emperor tamarin, shown above, has a unique mustache and beard. Golden lion tamarins, below, were once kept as pets because of their beautiful fur.

Coats of many colors

Marmosets and tamarins are known for their brightly colored, spiked fur. Some have bushy white fur on top of their head and ears. Others have long whiskers that look like a mustache! Golden lion tamarins have long, reddish orange fur that makes them look like small lions.

Sharing responsibility

In most primate families, the mother cares for her **offspring**, or babies, by carrying them all day. In marmoset and tamarin families, however, the father carries the babies. The young primates cling to the fur on his back with their hands and feet. They only climb onto their mother to **nurse**, or drink milk from her body.

Tiny primates

Pygmy marmosets are small enough to fit in the palm of your hand. They use different sounds to communicate with their troop. Some of their calls are so high pitched that humans cannot hear them. Pygmy marmosets live in families of four to fifteen members. Only one female in the group has babies, and the others help raise her young.

How are people different?

Although humans are related to apes, monkeys, and lemurs, there are many differences between us and other primates. Our brain is larger than that of other primates. We can learn to speak different languages, play musical instruments, and read books. Humans do not live in trees as other primates do, and we do not have thick fur covering our body. Can you think of any other ways in which you are different from other primates?

Walking upright

Humans are **bipedal**. We walk upright on two legs all the time, whereas most other primates use all four limbs for walking. Our legs are longer than our arms, and long legs help us take long strides when we walk. Our feet are **arched**, or curved, on the bottom to help make walking easier.

Some people have learned a lot about primates by studying them in their habitat. This woman and chimpanzee know each other well.

Primates in danger

The biggest threat to primates in the wild is the loss of their habitat. Most primates live in forests. They need trees and plants for shelter and food. When people cut down trees to build houses or grow crops, many primates lose their homes. Primates that have lost their habitat often cannot find food, and they eat crops planted by farmers. The farmers consider these animals pests and shoot them.

Human enemies

Poachers hunt primates illegally. They kill mother apes and sell the babies as pets. In some countries, people buy primate meat, skins, and fur. Some people pay a lot of money for primate souvenirs and meat, so poachers continue to kill many animals.

Protection for primates

Many people are helping primates by providing them with **sanctuaries**, or safe places in which to live. Some countries have banned the hunting of primates and created national parks where these animals can live safely.

Young orangutans that are taken from their mother often die from loneliness soon afterward.

Mountain gorillas are in danger of being killed by poachers, who sell gorilla hands and skulls to tourists.

Words to know

amplify To make larger or more powerful

body language Postures, gestures, and facial expressions used to show feelings

brachiation A way of moving around by swinging from one handhold to another

energy The power to do things

evolve To change or develop slowly over time

facial expression A face that a primate makes to show thoughts or feelings

gesture A hand or body movement used for communication

gland A body part that releases a substance

ischial callosities Thick pads of skin on a primate's buttocks

knuckle-walk To walk on all four limbs, supporting the upper body on the knuckles

long call A loud noise made by a primate to announce a claim on territory

opposable thumb The thumb on a primate's hand that allows the animal to pick up and hold objects

predator An animal that kills and eats other animals

prehensile Describing a body part that is used for grasping objects

prey (n) An animal that is hunted and eaten by another animal; (v) to hunt an animal

reproductive system The parts of the body that are necessary for making babies

silverback An adult male gorilla that has gray or silver hair on its back

three-dimensional Describing something that has three dimensions, or depths

Index

1 2 3 4 5 6 7 8 9 0 Printed in the U.S.A. 8 7 6 5 4 3 2 1 0 9